Certified Information Privacy Professional (dcpp-01) Exam Practice Questions & Dumps

Exam Practice Questions for dcpp-01
LATEST VERSION

Presented by: Quantic Books

About Quantic Books:

Quantic Books is a publishing house based in Princeton, New Jersey, USA. , a platform that is accessible online as well as locally, which gives power to educational content, erudite collection, poetry & many other book genres. We make it easy for writers & authors to get their books designed, published, promoted, and sell professionally on worldwide scale with eBook + Print distribution. Quantic Books is now distributing books worldwide.

Note: Find answers of the questions at the last of the book.

QUESTION 1

APEC privacy framework envisages common principles such as Notice, Collection limitation, Use Limitation, Access and Correction, Security/Safeguards, and Accountability. But it differs from the EU Data Protection Directive in which of the below aspect?

A. APEC privacy framework does not deal with the usage of personal information
B. APEC privacy framework does not mandate the binding treaties or directives for member countries
C. APEC privacy framework does not have a provision for co-operation between privacy enforcement agencies of members
D. APEC privacy framework does not deal with e-commerce

Section: Privacy Principles and Laws

QUESTION 2

A multinational company with operations in several parts within EU and outside EU, involves international data transfer of both its employees and customers. In some of its EU branches, which are relatively larger in size, the organization has a works council. Most of the data transferred is personal, and some of the data that the organization collects is sensitive in nature, the processing of some of which is also outsourced to its branches in Asian countries.

Which of the following **are not** mandatory pre-requisite before transferring sensitive personal data to its Asian branches?

A. Notifying the data subject
B. Conducting risk assessment for the processing involved
C. Determining adequacy status of the country
D. Self-certifying to Safe Harbor practices and reporting to Federal Trade Commission

QUESTION 3

A multinational company with operations in several parts within EU and outside EU, involves international data transfer of both its employees and customers. In some of its EU branches, which are relatively larger in size, the organization has a works council. Most of the data transferred is personal, and some of the data that the organization collects is sensitive in nature, the processing of some of which is also outsourced to its branches in Asian countries.

For the outsourced work of its customers' data processing, in order to initiate data transfer to another organizations outside EU, which is the most appropriate among the following?

A. The vendor (data importer) in the third country, and not the exporter is responsible to put in place suitable model contractual clauses, and hence the exporter does not need to take any action.
B. Since the data is processed by the vendor outside the EU, the EU directive does not apply and hence there are no legal concerns
C. The data exporter needs to initiate model contractual clauses after obtaining approvals from data protection commissioner and have the vendor be a signatory on the same as data importer
D. The data importer need to notify about the transfer to data protection commissioner in the destination country and exporter need to similarly notify in the EU country of origin

Section: Privacy Principles and Laws

QUESTION 4

With reference to APEC privacy framework, when personal information is to be transferred to another person or organization, whether domestically or internationally, "the__should obtain the consent of the individual and exercise due diligence and take reasonable steps to ensure that the recipient person or organization will protect the information consistently with APEC information privacy principles".

A. Personal Information Owner
B. Personal Information Controller
C. Personal Information Processor
D. Personal Information Auditor

QUESTION 5

Which of the following statements are true about the privacy statement of an organization?

A. Content of the online privacy statement of an organization will depend upon the applicable laws, and may need to address requirements across geographical boundaries and legal jurisdictions
B. As per privacy laws generally it is mandatory to mention the phone contact details of the owner of organization in the online privacy statement where customers can reach out in case of a grievance or incident
C. Online privacy statement is an instrument to demonstrate to stakeholders how the organization gathers, uses, discloses, and manages personal data
D. India's Information Technology (Amendment) Act, 2008 does not require that privacy policy be published on the website

Section: Privacy Principles and Laws

QUESTION 6

Please select the **incorrect** statement in context of "Online Privacy":

A. A person's act of 'Selective disclosure" (of themselves) in an online environment
B. A person's concern over usage of information that were collected during an online activity
C. A person's control over collection of information during an online activity
D. A person's concern on the software licensing agreement they sign with any organization

Section: Privacy Principles and Laws

QUESTION 7

Select the element(s) of APEC cross border privacy rules system from the following list:

i. self-assessment
ii. compliance review
iii. recognition/acceptance by APEC members
iv. dispute resolution and enforcement Please select correct option:

A. i, ii and iii
B. ii, iii, and iv
C. i, iii and iv
D. i, ii, iii and iv

Section: Privacy Principles and Laws

QUESTION 8

A ministry under government of India plans to collect citizens' information related to their education, medical condition, economic status, caste and religion. As per the privacy requirements mentioned under Sec 43A of IT (Amendment) Act, 2008, the citizens' 'Consent' would be mandatory for which of the following elements before their collection?

A. Educational records
B. Medical condition
C. Caste and religion
D. Sec 43A may not be applicable

Section: Privacy Principles and Laws

QUESTION 9

XYZ is a successful startup that acquired a respectable size & scale of operations in last 3 years, handling business process services for small & medium scale enterprises, largely in US & Europe. They are at the stage of closing a deal with a new banking client and working out the details of privacy related obligations in contract. Ensuring effective enforcement of which of the below listed privacy principles is client's accountability, even after outsourcing its loan approval process to XYZ?

I. Notice
II. Choice and Consent
III. Collection Limitation
IV. Use Limitation
V. Access and Correction
VI. Security
VII. Disclosure to third Party

Please select the correct set of principles from below listed options:

A. None of the above, since they are outsourcing the work to XYZ who will carry the liability going forward
B. All except V and VI
C. All except III
D. All of the above listed privacy principles

Section: Privacy Principles and Laws

QUESTION 10

Which of the following categories of information are generally protected under privacy laws?

A. Personally Identifiable Information (PII)
B. Sensitive Personal Information (SPI)
C. Trademark, copyright and patent information
D. Organizations' confidential business information

Section: Privacy Principles and Laws

QUESTION 11

A US IT company has created a cloud based application for Canadian consumers only, with servers located in Vancouver, Canada. The application allows its users to publish their short stories, essays or e-books. The purpose of the application, i.e. literary work, is clearly stated in the terms and conditions which are mandatorily acknowledged by each user.

With respect to this application, the company must ensure compliance with:

A. PIPEDA
B. US Consumer Privacy Bill of Rights
C. EU Data Protection Directive
D. None of the above

Section: Privacy Principles and Laws

QUESTION 12

Indian constitution does not expressly provide for the "right to privacy" to its citizens. However, there were various judicial pronouncements of the apex court which finally established the "right to privacy" as a fundamental right subsumed under Article 21 of the constitution of India. Article 21 inter alia provides and protects the

_____.

A. Right to Life and Personal liberty
B. Right to Opportunity
C. Right to Freedom of Speech and Expression
D. Right to Equality before law

Section: Privacy Principles and Laws

QUESTION 13

Which among the following is the Canadian privacy law?

A. COPPA
B. PIPEDA
C. HIPAA
D. IT Act of Canada

Section: Privacy Principles and Laws

QUESTION 14

ABC company is a large US based IT Company that provides a range of services to its clients. The company had developed a cloud based application providing end-to-end services for the medical industry. The application had three modules for:
-Patients
-Hospitals and Doctors
-Insurance and Pharmaceutical companies

Each of the modules was designed to be integrated with others depending on user's choice. For example, a patient could choose to share his/her medical history with his/her doctor (for medical advice) as well as insurance companies (for claims).

The application requires that all registered users of the application read and acknowledge the privacy policy. Additionally, users are required to identify the purpose for which they are providing any personal data in any of the modules. For example, a patient providing his/her medical history and current symptoms can select 'Medical Advice' as the purpose for the data being provided.

Few months ago, company launched new services in the applications namely, Business Analytics, Group Consultations, Insurance Policy purchase, and Medical Trials Management. The new services used all existing data collected over the years from users. The Company's clients/users are based only in three geographical locations - United States, European Union and India. Additionally, to facilitate better performance of its application, the company established one datacenter each in US, Germany and India for its operations. Each of the datacenter provides the following:
-US Datacenter - Storage of data for US based users only
-Germany Datacenter - Storage of data for EU based users only
-India Datacenter - Storage of data for India based users and alternate

site for US and Germany Datacenters (used as part of global load balancing)

-Services of a cloud service provider are leveraged in US as a Disaster Recovery (DR) site for Indian Datacenter

Recently, the company's Application Support Desk has started receiving user complaints related to unsolicited communications. These complaints have warranted a review of company's privacy policies as well as practices.

The use of all user data for business analytics would be in direct conflict with which of the following privacy principles?

A. Access and Correction
B. Collection Limitation
C. Data Quality
D. Use Limitation

Section: Privacy Principles and Laws

QUESTION 15

As per GDPR, the adequacy decision is taken the European Commission based on its findings and assessment of privacy laws of the third country, territory, sector, etc. The_is required to provide the Commission with an opinion for the assessment of the adequacy of the level of protection in a third country or international organization, including for the assessment whether a third country, a territory or one or more specified sectors within that third country, or an international organization.

A. European Data Protection Board
B. Article 29 Working Party
C. Lead Supervisory Authority
D. Convention 108 Council

Section: Privacy Principles and Laws

QUESTION 16

As per Article 6 of General Data Protection Regulation, 2016, which of the following is not a lawful ground of processing personal data?

A. Performance of Contract
B. Legal Obligation
C. Legitimate Interest
D. Consent
E. Vital Interest
F. All of them are lawful grounds of processing personal data

Section: Privacy Principles and Laws

QUESTION 17

"As per Indian laws, any information that is freely available or accessible in public domain cannot be regarded as sensitive personal data or information." Please state if this statement is True or False.

A. True
B. False

Section: Privacy Principles and Laws

QUESTION 18

The Information Technology (Reasonable Security Practices And Procedures and Sensitive Data or Information) Rules, 2011 incorporate which of the following privacy concepts and principles:

i. Collection Limitation
ii. Accountability
iii. Right to be forgotten

iv. Purpose Limitation
v. Access and correction

A. i, ii, iii and iv
B. I, ii, iv and v
C. I, iii, iv and v
D. All the above

Section: Privacy Principles and Laws

QUESTION 19

While transferring personal data from an EU member nation to a third country which is not deemed adequate as per EU's assessment, which of the following step is not relevant?

A. Signing of model contractual clauses
B. Notifying or taking approval from the Data Protection Authority
C. Assessing the appropriateness of safeguards and measures adopted by the importing organization commensurate to the sensitivity of data being transferred
D. Harmonizing data protection legislations between the two geographies

Section: Privacy Principles and Laws

QUESTION 20

The term "Data Handlers" is synonymous with which of the following privacy legislations?

A. South Korea's Personal Information Protection Act
B. Digital Privacy Act, 2015
C. Federal Data Protection Act, Germany (BDSG)
D. Child online protection Act, 1998

Section: Privacy Principles and Laws

QUESTION 21

The Qatar Concerning Privacy and Protection of Personal Data Act, 2016 applies to:

A. Only personal data that is electronically processed
B. Only personal data that is manually processed
C. Personal data that is electronically or manually processed

Section: Privacy Principles and Laws

QUESTION 22

"Any company joining the EU-US Privacy Shield has to self-certify to the

US Department of Commerce and make a public commitment to the

same". Is this statement True or False?

A. True
B. False

Section: Privacy Principles and Laws

QUESTION 23

An Indian company provides BPM services to a US based health insurance company. One rogue of the employees of the Indian company exported patient data of the customers of the insurance company and provided it to another US based insurance company. Although the employee was charged for theft, the company and its executives also faced legal proceedings in India because (please select the most appropriate possible reason):

A. They did not conduct background verification of individuals.
B. They allowed access to sensitive personal information to employees of the company.
C. They did not implement reasonable security practices for data protection.
D. They did not implement data loss prevention tools to prevent such actions.

Section: Privacy Principles and Laws

QUESTION 24

XYZ Inc of USA has setup a captive back office operations center in India. The captive is registered as a separate legal entity by the name XYZ India Private Limited and provides services only to XYZ Inc by catering its technology support needs. During the process of providing services, the Indian entity does not receive any customer information of the XYZ Inc. However, information such as financial information and biometric information etc. of the employees of XYZ India is shared with the XYZ Inc.

What necessary steps need to be taken before actual sharing of the aforesaid information happens?

1. Seek consent from the employees of XYZ India before sharing the information;
2. A lawful contract between the XYZ Inc and XYZ India regarding the terms of sharing and data protection measures to be taken, with the obligation on XYZ Inc of not sharing the received information further without permission from Indian entity;
3. The XYZ Inc should agree to provide better or at-par level of data protection as prescribed in the IT (Amendment) Act, 2008;
4. The country in which the XYZ Inc is located should ensure better or same level of data protection as prescribed in the IT (Amendment) Act, 2008

A. 1 and 2

B. 1, 2 and 3

C. 2 and 3

D. 1 and 4

Section: Privacy Principles and Laws

QUESTION 25

According to The Information Technology (Reasonable Security Practices And Procedures and Sensitive Data or Information) Rules, 2011, which of the following does not fall under the category of Sensitive Personal Data or Information?

A. Sexual orientation
B. Password
C. Medical records and history
D. Religious Beliefs

Section: Privacy Principles and Laws

QUESTION 26

Japanese Act on the Protection of Personal Information or APPI applies to:

A. Applies to the use of a personal information for businesses
B. Applies to the use of personal information by government entities
C. Both A and B

Section: Privacy Principles and Laws

QUESTION 27

Rising economic value of personal information has stressed the need for a comprehensive_____legislation in India.

A. Right to Internet
B. Privacy
C. Right to Information
D. Dispute resolution

Section: Privacy Fundamentals

QUESTION 28

Which of the following **does not** fall under the category of Personal Financial Information (PFI)?

A. Credit card number with expiry date
B. Bank account Information
C. Loan account Information
D. Income tax return file acknowledgement number

Section: Privacy Fundamentals

QUESTION 29

If XYZ & Co. collects, stores and processes personal information of living persons, electronically in a structured filing system, then XYZ could be a:

A. Data Processor
B. Data Controller
C. Data Subject
D. Either A or B

Section: Privacy Fundamentals

QUESTION 30

Which of the following **doesn't contribute, or contributes the least**, to the growing data privacy challenges in today's digital age?

A. Social media
B. Mass surveillance
C. Use of secure wireless connections
D. Increase in digitization of personal information

Section: Privacy Fundamentals

QUESTION 31

Choose the correct statement:
Projects like DNA profiling, UIDAI, collection of individual's statistics, etc.

A. Are executed with a sole aim to ensure that privacy of individuals is maintained
B. Have been initiated to provide services to citizens for maintaining their online privacy only
C. Have raised the need for a comprehensive privacy legislation at national level
D. Have enforced a privacy legislation at national level

Section: Privacy Fundamentals

QUESTION 32

In the history of human evolution, erection of walls and fences around one's living spaces is interpreted as arrival of which type of privacy consciousness?

A. Data privacy
B. Physical privacy
C. Organizational privacy
D. Communication privacy

Section: Privacy Fundamentals

QUESTION 33

What does PHI stand for, as per HIPAA/ HITECH?

A. Personal healthcare information
B. Public health information
C. Protected health information
D. Personal health information

Section: Privacy Fundamentals

QUESTION 34

Which of the following best describes the practice of delivering specifically targeted advertisements to users, based on their online activities?

A. Digital Marketing
B. Behavioral Advertising
C. Tracking
D. Profiling

Section: Privacy Fundamentals

QUESTION 35

Which US Federal Law lays the framework for provision of data stored on servers outside US territory?

A. Clarifying Lawful Overseas Use of Data Act, 2018
B. Compelling Lawful Overseas Use of Data Act, 2018
C. Overseas Lawful Data Corporation Act, 2018
D. Remote Lawful Overseas Use of Data Act, 2016

Section: Privacy Fundamentals

QUESTION 36

On which date is the Data Privacy Day or Data Protection Day celebrated?

A. 27th January
B. 28th January
C. 28th June
D. 16th November

Section: Privacy Fundamentals

QUESTION 37

Which of the following should be the part of the Privacy Policy of any organization?

A. Applicable Privacy Principles
B. Contact details of senior management
C. Definition of Personal Information and associated categories
D. Details of all the privacy incidents that have occurred in the past

Section: Privacy Fundamentals

QUESTION 38

Data processing includes which of the following operations:

A. Collecting
B. Transmitting
C. Storing
D. Disclosing
E. All of the above

Section: Privacy Fundamentals

QUESTION 39

Section 43A of the Information Technology (Amendment) Act, 2008 holds_____accountable for having reasonable security practices and procedures in place to protection sensitive personal data.

A. Government
B. Body Corporates
C. Government and body corporates alike
D. none of the above

Section: Privacy Fundamentals

QUESTION 40

Which of the following is not in line with the Modern definition of Consent?

A. Consent is taken by clear and affirmative action.
B. Consent Should be Bundled in Nature.
C. Consenting individual should have the ability to withdraw consent.
D. Purpose of Processing should be informed to the individual before consenting.

Section: Privacy Fundamentals

QUESTION 41

Which of the following best defines a 'Data Subject'?

A. One who provides his/her personal information for availing any service
B. One who processes the data/information of individuals for providing necessary services
C. Corporate entity whose confidential information is shared with business partners

Section: Privacy Fundamentals

QUESTION 42

Which among the following organizations **does not** issue a privacy seal?

A. EuroPriSe
B. BBBOnline
C. Transaction Guard
D. WebTrust

Section: Privacy Technologies and Organization Ecosystem

QUESTION 43

As part of the environment scanning to identify security risks to personal information, which of the following environments **would be least** relevant for the organization?

A. Organization's own environment
B. Service provider's environment
C. Client's environment
D. Government agencies' environment which seek lawful access to personal data

Section: Privacy Technologies and Organization Ecosystem

QUESTION 44

Which of the following could be considered as triggers for updating privacy policy?

A. Regulatory changes
B. Privacy breach
C. Change in service provider for an established business process
D. Recruitment of more employees

Section: Privacy Technologies and Organization Ecosystem

QUESTION 45

As a newly-appointed privacy officer of an IT company gearing up for DSCI's privacy certification, you are trying to understand what data elements are involved in each of the business process, function and if these data elements can be classified as sensitive personal information.

What is being accomplished with this effort?

A. Organization to get "Visibility" over its exposure to sensitive personal information
B. It is a part of the annual exercise per the organization's privacy policy/ processes
C. Information security controls for confidential information being reviewed
D. Gathering inputs to restructure privacy function

Section: Privacy Technologies and Organization Ecosystem

QUESTION 46

From the following list, identify the technology aspects that are specially designed for upholding the privacy:

i. Data minimization
ii. Intrusion prevention system
iii. Data scrambling
iv. Data loss prevention
v. Data portability
vi. Data obfuscation
vii. Data encryption
viii. Data mirroring

Please select the correct set of aspects from below options:

A. Only i., iii., vii. and viii
B. Only i., ii., iii., vii. and viii
C. Only i., ii., vi. and vii
D. Only ii., v., vi., vii. and viii

Section: Privacy Technologies and Organization Ecosystem

QUESTION 47

With respect to privacy notice, what are the responsibilities of data controller?

A. Providing the notice before or during data collection
B. Identifying and communication the purposes for which data will be collected, used, and disclosed
C. Providing notice after the data collection
D. Providing notice at every instance of data processing

Section: Privacy Technologies and Organization Ecosystem

QUESTION 48

A privacy lead assessor assessing your company for DSCI's privacy certification gets to know that your payroll process has been outsourced to a third party service provider. So, he/she is reviewing your contract with that service provider to ascertain which privacy related clauses are incorporated in the contract.

What could be the possible reasons for reviewing the contract?

A. Possible violation of 'Collection Limitation'
B. Possible violation of 'Use Limitation'
C. Risk of data subjects directly reaching to service provider
D. Data security controls in third party provider's environment

Section: Privacy Technologies and Organization Ecosystem

QUESTION 49

Which of the following mechanisms or steps are likely to be taken by an organization for implementing privacy program?

i Deploying physical and technology safeguards to protect personal information assets
ii. Privacy consideration in product and service design
iii. Privacy implementation to focus only on projects impacted by privacy breaches
iv. Benchmarking against industry peers' privacy implementation
v. Installing privacy enhancing tools and technologies for the projects

dealing with organization's intellectual property Please select the correct

set of statements from the below options:

A. All
B. All except iii
C. Only i, and ii
D. Only i, ii and iv

Section: Privacy Technologies and Organization Ecosystem

QUESTION 50

Which of the following could be considered as the most beneficial aspect of implementing Privacy Enhancing Technologies or Tools (PETs)?

A. Improves the quality of the information.
B. Reduces audit, supervisory and management costs.
C. Increases users' control over their personal data.
D. Ensures security by design in all products and services.

Section: Privacy Technologies and Organization Ecosystem

QUESTION 51

Which among the following would not be characteristic of a good privacy notice?

A. Easy to understand
B. Clear and concise
C. Comprehensive – explaining all the possible scenarios and processing details making the notice lengthy
D. Multilingual

Section: Privacy Technologies and Organization Ecosystem

QUESTION 52

A global Business Process Management (BPM) organization based in India, headquartered in the US is in receipt of a Request for Proposal (RFP) for a potential deal. The privacy function in this company has just got formulated.

Which of the following stage would be most effective for sales team to involve privacy function?

A. RFP response stage
B. Post-RFP stage once the BPM organization is selected as one of the potential service providers
C. During service provider evaluation stage based on RFP response, and face-to-face reviews of the service provider
D. During contract negotiation stage

Section: Privacy Technologies and Organization Ecosystem

QUESTION 53

Methods for de-identification can be classified into two types:

A. Statistical and Heuristic Methods
B. Human and Machine Methods
C. Advanced and Compilation Methods
D. None of the above

Section: Privacy Technologies and Organization Ecosystem

QUESTION 54

In which of the following stages of the personal information life cycle, should the security aspects be considered?

1. Collection
2. Maintenance
3. Distribution
4. Disposition

A. 1,2 and 3
B. 2, 3 and 4
C. 2 and 3
D. 1,2,3 and 4

Section: Privacy Technologies and Organization Ecosystem

ANSWERS

1. Correct Answer: B
2. Correct Answer: D
3. Correct Answer: D
4. Correct Answer: B
Reference: https://iapp.org/news/a/gdpr-matchup-the-apec-privacy-framework-and-cross-borde-privacy-rules/

5. Correct Answer: A
Reference: https://en.wikipedia.org/wiki/Privacy_policy

6. Correct Answer: C
7. Correct Answer: C
8. Correct Answer: B
9. Correct Answer: C
10. Correct Answer: A
11. Correct Answer: D
12. Correct Answer: A

Reference:
   Article 21 of the Constitution of India, 1950 provides that, "No person shall be deprived of his life or personal liberty except according to procedure established by law.
Reference:
https://www.google.com/search?q=article+21+of+indian+constit
ution&rlz=1C1CHBF_enPK808PK808&oq=article+21+of+india&a
qs=chrome.0.0j69i57j0l4.3344j0j7&sourceid=chrome&ie=UTF-8

13. Correct Answer: B
14. Correct Answer: D
Reference: http://oecdprivacy.org/#quality

15. Correct Answer: A
Reference:
https://books.google.com.pk/books?id=rKXaDwAAQBAJ&pg=P
A141&lpg=PA141&dq=GDPR+is+required+to+provide+the+Com
mission+with+an+opinion+for+the+assessment+of+the+adequa
cy+of+the+level+of+protection+in+a+third+country+or+internati
onal+organization,+including+for+the+assessment+whether+a+
third+country,+a+territory+or+one+or+more+specified+sectors
+within+that+third+country,+or+an+international

+organization&source=bl&ots=iTGUI_dS9C&sig=ACfU3U1_Q4w
LavcnbA58JvJ8ek3PZ6YVqg&hl=en&sa=X&ved=2ahUKEwjk4NT
nyp_pAhXCRBUIHXqlDj4Q6AEw
DHoECBQQAQ#v=onepage&q=GDPR%20is%20required%20to
%20provide%20the%20Commission%20wi
th%20an%20opinion%20for%20the%20assessment%
20of%20the%20adequacy%20of%20the%20level%20of%20prote
ction%20in%20a%20third%20country%20or%20international%2
0organization%2C%20including%
20for%20the%20assessment%20whether%20a%20third%20cou
ntry%2C%20a%20territory%20or%20one%20or%20more%20spe
cified%20sectors%20within%
20that%20third%20country%2C%20or%20an%20international%
20organization&f=false

16. Correct Answer: A
Reference: https://ico.org.uk/for-organisations/guide-to-data-
protection/guide-to-the-general-data-protection-regulation-
gdpr/lawful-basis-for-processing/

17. Correct Answer: A
/Reference:
Reference: https://www.linklaters.com/en/insights/data-
protected/data-protected---india

18. Correct Answer: B
19. Correct Answer: C
20. Correct Answer: A
Reference: https://www.smaato.com/blog/inside-south-korea-
personal-information-protection-act-gdpr/

21. Correct Answer: A
Reference:
https://www.motc.gov.qa/en/documents/document/qatar-
issues-personal-data-privacy-law-5

22. Correct Answer: A
Reference: https://www.privacytrust.com/privacyshield/

23. Correct Answer: C
24. Correct Answer: C
25. Correct Answer: B
Reference: https://www.mondaq.com/india/data-
protection/626190/information-technology-reasonable-security-
practices-and-procedures-and-sensitive-personal- data-or-

information-rules-2011

26. Correct Answer: A
Reference: https://www.dataguidance.com/notes/japan-data-protection-overview

27. Correct Answer: A
28. Correct Answer: D
29. Correct Answer: B
30. Correct Answer: A
31. Correct Answer: B
32. Correct Answer: D
33. Correct Answer: C
Reference:
https://en.wikipedia.org/wiki/Health_Insurance_Portability_and_Accountability_Act

34. Correct Answer: B
Reference: https://www.priv.gc.ca/en/privacy-topics/technology/online-privacy-tracking-cookies/tracking-and-ads/gl_ba_1112/

35. Correct Answer: A
Reference: https://en.wikipedia.org/wiki/CLOUD_Act

36. Correct Answer: B
Reference: https://en.wikipedia.org/wiki/Data_Privacy_Day

37. Correct Answer: C
Reference: https://www.privacypolicies.com/blog/privacy-policy-template/

38. Correct Answer: C
Reference: https://www.mbaknol.com/management-information-systems/data-processing-operations/

39. Correct Answer: A
Reference: https://www.mondaq.com/india/data-protection/626190/information-technology-reasonable-security-practices-and-procedures-and-sensitive-personal-data-or-information-rules-2011

40. Correct Answer: B
Reference: https://en.wikipedia.org/wiki/Consent

41. Correct Answer: A
Reference: https://www.temos-worldwide.com/data-privacy-statement.aspx

42. Correct Answer: C
43. Correct Answer: D
44. Correct Answer: A
45. Correct Answer: C
46. Correct Answer: C
47. Correct Answer: B
48. Correct Answer: A
49. Correct Answer: B
50. Correct Answer: C
51. Correct Answer: A
Reference: https://gdpr.eu/privacy-notice/

52. Correct Answer: D
53. Correct Answer: B
Reference
https://bmcmedresmethodol.biomedcentral.com/articles/10.1186/1471-2288-12-109

54. Correct Answer: B
Reference:
https://en.wikipedia.org/wiki/Information_lifecycle_management

www.ingramcontent.com/pod-product-compliance
Lightning Source LLC
LaVergne TN
LVHW051649050326
832903LV00034B/4767